THIS BOOK BELONGS TO:

Omid
Omid
Omid

Shop our other books at
www.sillyslothpress.com

For questions and customer service, email us at
support@sillyslothpress.com

JOKE 1

KNOCK, KNOCK.
WHO'S THERE?
LOCK.
LOCK WHO?
LOCK WHO IT IS,
AFTER ALL THIS TIME!

JOKE 2

KNOCK, KNOCK.
WHO'S THERE?
FOSSIL.
FOSSIL WHO?
FOSSIL LAST TIME,
PLEASE LET ME IN!

JOKE 3

KNOCK, KNOCK.
WHO'S THERE?
ROBIN.
ROBIN WHO?
ROBIN YOU,
NOW EMPTY YOUR POCKETS!

JOKE 4

KNOCK, KNOCK.
WHO'S THERE?
DON JUAN
DON JUAN WHO?
DON JUAN TO DO
MY HOMEWORK.

JOKE 5

KNOCK, KNOCK.
WHO'S THERE?
FIDDLE.
FIDDLE?
FIDDLE MAKE ME HAPPY
IF YOU OPEN THIS DOOR!

JOKE 6

KNOCK, KNOCK.
WHO'S THERE?
RABBIT
RABBIT WHO?
RABBIT CAREFULLY.
IT'S A GIFT.

JOKE 7

KNOCK, KNOCK.
WHO'S THERE?
IONA.
IONA WHO?
IONA NEW TOY!

JOKE 8

KNOCK, KNOCK.
WHO'S THERE?
DOZEN.
DOZEN WHO?
DOZEN SOMEONE
WANT TO OPEN THE DOOR?

JOKE 9

KNOCK, KNOCK!
WHO'S THERE?
CUMIN.
CUMIN WHO?
CUMIN SIDE,
IT'S COZY IN HERE!

JOKE 10

KNOCK, KNOCK.
WHO'S THERE?
KEANU.
KEANU WHO?
KEANU LET ME IN,
IT'S FREEZING OUT HERE.

JOKE 11

KNOCK, KNOCK.
WHO'S THERE?
HADA!
HADA WHO?
HAD A WONDERFUL DAY,
HOW WAS YOURS?

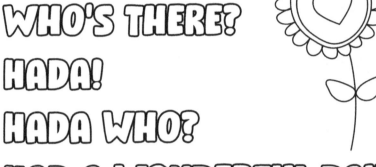

JOKE 12

KNOCK, KNOCK!
WHO'S THERE?
DEDUCT.
DEDUCT WHO?
DONALD DEDUCT

JOKE 13

KNOCK, KNOCK.
WHO'S THERE?
DWAYNE.
DWAYNE WHO?
DWAYNE THE BATHTUB,
I'M DWOWNING!

JOKE 14

KNOCK, KNOCK.
WHO'S THERE?
EGG.
EGG WHO?
EGGSCITED TO HEAR
ANOTHER JOKE?

JOKE 15

KNOCK, KNOCK.
WHO'S THERE?
WOODEN SHOE.
WOODEN SHOE WHO?
WOODEN SHOE
LIKE TO KNOW?

JOKE 16

KNOCK, KNOCK.
WHO'S THERE?
EMMA.
EMMA WHO?
EMMA
GROW GREY HAIR
WAITING FOR
YOU TO OPEN UP!

JOKE 17

KNOCK, KNOCK!
WHO'S THERE?
IVORY.
IVORY WHO?
IVORY STRONG
LIKE SUPERMAN!

JOKE 18

KNOCK, KNOCK.
WHO'S THERE?
ABBY.
ABBY WHO?
ABBY BIRTHDAY TO YOU!

KNOCK, KNOCK.
WHO'S THERE?
ALFIE.
ALFIE WHO?
ALFIE AWFUL IF YOU
DON'T LET ME IN!

KNOCK, KNOCK!
WHO'S THERE?
BEAN.
BEAN WHO?
BEAN A WHILE SINCE
I TOLD YOU
A KNOCK-KNOCK JOKE.

JOKE 21

KNOCK, KNOCK
WHO'S THERE?
A LEAF.
A LEAF WHO?
A LEAF YOU ALONE
IF YOU LEAF ME ALONE.

JOKE 22

KNOCK, KNOCK.
WHO'S THERE?
COWS.
COWS WHO?
COWS GO MOO
NOT WHO!

JOKE 23

KNOCK, KNOCK.
WHO'S THERE?
TANK.
TANK WHO?
YOU'RE WELCOME.

JOKE 24

KNOCK, KNOCK
WHO'S THERE?
LUKE'S
LUKE'S WHO?
LUKE'S LIKE IT'S
GOING TO RAIN,
YOU SHOULD LET ME IN.

JOKE 25

KNOCK, KNOCK!
WHO'S THERE?
IRMA.
IRMA WHO?
IRMA BIG KID NOW.

JOKE 26

KNOCK, KNOCK.
WHO'S THERE?
BOBBY BUN PICKLES.
BOBBY BUN PICKLES WHO?
EXACTLY HOW MANY
BOBBY BUN PICKLES
DO YOU KNOW?

JOKE 27

KNOCK, KNOCK.
WHO'S THERE?
MEG.
MEG WHO?
MEG UP YOUR MIND.
ARE YOU GOING TO LET
ME IN OR NOT?

JOKE 28

KNOCK, KNOCK.
WHO'S THERE?
HAWAII.
HAWAII WHO?
I'M FINE, HAWAII YOU?

JOKE 29

KNOCK, KNOCK.
WHO'S THERE?
NOAH.
NOAH WHO?
NOAH GOOD PLACE
TO EAT?

JOKE 30

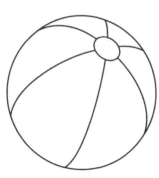

KNOCK, KNOCK!
WHO'S THERE?
BELLA.
BELLA WHO?
I'M THE BELLA THE BALL.

JOKE 31

KNOCK, KNOCK.
WHO'S THERE?
AVENUE.
AVENUE WHO?
AVENUE HEARD
THIS JOKE BEFORE?

JOKE 32

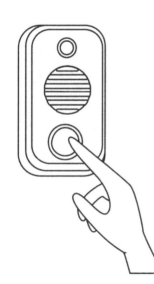

KNOCK, KNOCK
WHO'S THERE?
NOBEL.
NOBEL WHO?
NOBEL...THAT'S
WHY I KNOCKED!

JOKE 33

KNOCK, KNOCK!
WHO'S THERE?
HANDSOME.
HANDSOME WHO?
HANDSOME COOKIES
TO ME PLEASE.

JOKE 34

KNOCK, KNOCK
WHO'S THERE?
ODYSSEUS.
ODYSSEUS WHO?
ODYSSEUS
THE LAST STRAW!

JOKE 35

KNOCK, KNOCK.
WHO'S THERE?
EUROPE.
EUROPE WHO?
NO, YOU'RE A POO!

JOKE 36

KNOCK, KNOCK.
WHO'S THERE?
CUPID!
CUPID WHO?
CUPID QUIET IN THERE.

JOKE 37

KNOCK, KNOCK.
WHO'S THERE?
HARRY.
HARRY WHO?
HARRY UP AND UNLOCK
THIS DOOR!

JOKE 38

KNOCK, KNOCK.
WHO'S THERE?
CANOE
CANOE WHO?
CANOE OPEN THE DOOR?

JOKE 39

KNOCK, KNOCK
WHO'S THERE?
POLL.
POLL WHO?
POLICE!

JOKE 40

KNOCK, KNOCK.
WHO'S THERE?
ALEX.
ALEX WHO?
HEY, ALEX THE QUESTIONS
AROUND HERE!

JOKE 41

KNOCK, KNOCK.
WHO'S THERE?
BARBIE.
BARBIE WHO?
BARBIE Q SAUCE!

JOKE 42

KNOCK, KNOCK.
WHO'S THERE?
FRANK.
FRANK WHO?
FRANK YOU FOR LISTENING
TO MY JOKES.

JOKE 43

KNOCK, KNOCK!
WHO'S THERE?
GROVE.
GROVER WHO?
GROVER THERE
AND GET ME A PIZZA SLICE.

JOKE 44

KNOCK, KNOCK.
WHO'S THERE?
ADA.
ADA WHO?
ADA SANDWICH
FOR DINNER!

KNOCK, KNOCK.
WHO'S THERE?
TOOTH.
TOOTH WHO?
TOOTH OR DARE!

KNOCK, KNOCK!
WHO'S THERE?
FRED.
FRED WHO!
WHO'S A FRED
OF GHOSTS?

JOKE 47

KNOCK, KNOCK.
WHO'S THERE?
JUNO.
JUNO WHO?
JUNO YOUR DOORBELL
IS BROKEN?

JOKE 48

KNOCK, KNOCK.
WHO'S THERE?
HIP.
HIP WHO?
HIPPOPOTAMUS.

JOKE 49

KNOCK, KNOCK.
WHO'S THERE?
ICE CREAM SODA.
ICE CREAM SODA WHO?
ICE CREAM SODA PEOPLE CAN HEAR ME!

JOKE 50

KNOCK, KNOCK.
WHO'S THERE?
I DID UP.
I DID UP WHO?
YOU DID A POO?

KNOCK, KNOCK.
WHO'S THERE?
BUTTER.
BUTTER WHO?
BUTTER OPEN
THIS DOOR!

KNOCK, KNOCK.
WHO'S THERE?
GANDHI.
GANDHI WHO?
GANDHI COME
OUT AND PLAY?

JOKE 53

KNOCK, KNOCK.
WHO'S THERE?
ORANGE.
ORANGE WHO?
ORANGE YOU GLAD
TO HEAR MY JOKES?

JOKE 54

KNOCK, KNOCK.
WHO'S THERE?
CASH.
CASH WHO?
NO THANKS,
I'D RATHER HAVE PEANUTS.

JOKE 55

KNOCK, KNOCK.
WHO'S THERE?
GOLIATH
GOLIATH WHO?
GOLIATH DOWN,
YOU SEEM SLEEPY.

JOKE 56

KNOCK, KNOCK.
WHO'S THERE?
YORK.
YORK WHO?
YORK BETTER
OPEN THIS DOOR!

JOKE 57

KNOCK, KNOCK.
WHO'S THERE?
FROSTBITE.
FROSTBITE WHO?
FROSTBITE YOUR FOOD,
THEN CHEW AND SWALLOW.

JOKE 58

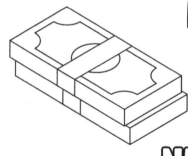

KNOCK, KNOCK
WHO'S THERE?
NICHOLAS.
NICHOLAS WHO?
A NICHOLAS NOT WORTH
MUCH MONEY ANYMORE.

JOKE 59

KNOCK, KNOCK.
WHO'S THERE?
WAITER.
WAITER WHO?
WAITER I GET
MY HANDS ON YOU!

JOKE 60

KNOCK, KNOCK.
WHO'S THERE?
BED.
BED WHO?
BED YOU CAN'T GUESS
WHAT I'M THINKING!

JOKE 61

KNOCK, KNOCK.
WHO'S THERE?
IRISH.
IRISH WHO?
IRISH YOU
AN AWESOME DAY!

JOKE 62

KNOCK, KNOCK.
WHO'S THERE?
RIOT.
RIOT WHO?
I AM RIOT ON TIME!

JOKE 63

KNOCK, KNOCK.
WHO'S THERE?
THERMOS.
THERMOS WHO?
THERMOS BE A WAY
TO OPEN THIS DOOR.

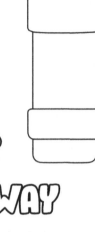

JOKE 64

KNOCK, KNOCK.
WHO'S THERE?
AMANDA.
AMANDA WHO?
A MAN DA REPAIR
YOUR DOORBELL!

JOKE 65

KNOCK, KNOCK.
WHO'S THERE?
OMAR.
OMAR WHO?
OMAR GOODNESS,
IT'S GREAT TO SEE YOU!

JOKE 66

KNOCK, KNOCK
WHO'S THERE?
ART.
ART WHO?
R2-D2!

JOKE 67

KNOCK, KNOCK.
WHO'S THERE?
NORMA LEE.
NORMA LEE WHO?
NORMA LEE I HAVE A KEY,
BUT I LOST IT.
WILL YOU LET ME IN?

JOKE 68

KNOCK, KNOCK!
WHO'S THERE?
YOURSELF.
YOURSELF WHO?
YOUR CELL PHONE'S
RINGING
YOU SHOULD ANSWER IT!

JOKE 69

KNOCK, KNOCK.
WHO'S THERE?
TYRONE.
TYRONE WHO?
TYRONE SHOELACES!

JOKE 70

KNOCK, KNOCK.
WHO'S THERE?
A HERD.
A HERD WHO?
A HERD YOU WERE HOME,
SO I CAME TO SAY HELLO!

JOKE 71

KNOCK, KNOCK.
WHO'S THERE?
HONEYDEW
HONEYDEW WHO?
HONEYDEW YOU WANT
TO OPEN THE DOOR?

JOKE 72

KNOCK, KNOCK.
WHO'S THERE?
CLAIRE.
CLAIRE WHO?
CLAIRE THE PATH,
I'M COMING IN!

JOKE 73

KNOCK, KNOCK
WHO'S THERE?
SNIFFMOP.
SNIFFMOP WHO?
GROSS, NO THANKS!

JOKE 74

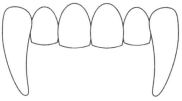

KNOCK, KNOCK.
WHO'S THERE?
FANGS.
FANGS WHO?
FANGS FOR ANSWERING
THE DOOR!

JOKE 75

KNOCK, KNOCK.
WHO'S THERE?
RHINO!
RHINO WHO?
RHINO MORE
KNOCK-KNOCK
JOKES THAN YOU!

JOKE 76

KNOCK, KNOCK.
WHO'S THERE?
ABE.
ABE WHO?
ABE C D E F...

JOKE 77

KNOCK, KNOCK
WHO'S THERE?
ANNIE.
ANNIE WHO?
ANNIE THING YOU CAN
DO I CAN BETTER!

JOKE 78

KNOCK, KNOCK.
WHO'S THERE?
GOOSE.
GOOSE WHO?
GOOSE WHO WANTS
TO COME INSIDE AGAIN!

JOKE 79

KNOCK, KNOCK!
WHO'S THERE?
PASTURE.
PASTURE WHO?
PASTURE BEDTIME ISN'T IT?

JOKE 80

KNOCK, KNOCK
WHO'S THERE?
I AM.
I AM WHO?
YOU DON'T KNOW
WHO YOU ARE?!

JOKE 81

KNOCK, KNOCK.
WHO'S THERE?
JAMAICA.
JAMAICA WHO?
JAMAICA SOME BURGERS?
I'M HUNGRY!

JOKE 82

KNOCK, KNOCK.
WHO'S THERE?
NOSE.
NOSE WHO?
I NOSE THE BEST
KNOCK-KNOCK JOKES!

JOKE 83

KNOCK, KNOCK.
WHO'S THERE?
SPELL.
SPELL WHO?
W-H-O

JOKE 84

KNOCK, KNOCK.
WHO'S THERE?
FRANCE.
FRANCE WHO?
FRANCE OF THE FAMILY!

JOKE 85

KNOCK, KNOCK.
WHO'S THERE?
AMARILLO.
AMARILLO WHO?
AMARILLO JOKESTER.

JOKE 86

KNOCK, KNOCK.
WHO'S THERE?
JAVA.
JAVA WHO?
JAVA DOG IN YOUR HOUSE?
I HEAR ONE BARKING!

JOKE 87

KNOCK, KNOCK.
WHO'S THERE?
ICY.
ICY WHO?
ICY YOU LOOKING
AT ME!

JOKE 88

KNOCK, KNOCK.
WHO'S THERE?
TAD.
TAD WHO?
TAD'S ALL, FOLKS!

JOKE 89

KNOCK, KNOCK.
WHO'S THERE?
OWLS SAY.
OWLS SAY WHO?
YES, YES THEY DO.

JOKE 90

KNOCK, KNOCK.
WHO'S THERE?
FORK.
FORK WHO?
FORK-GET IT,
I'M OUT OF HERE!

JOKE 91

KNOCK, KNOCK.
WHO'S THERE?
QUICHE.
QUICHE WHO?
CAN I HAVE A HUG
AND A QUICHE?

JOKE 92

KNOCK, KNOCK.
WHO'S THERE?
PHILIP.
PHILIP WHO?
PHILIP UP MY
GLASS PLEASE, I'M THIRSTY!

JOKE 93

KNOCK, KNOCK.
WHO'S THERE?
ICON.
ICON WHO?
ICON TELL MORE
KNOCK-KNOCK
JOKES THAN YOU CAN.

JOKE 94

KNOCK, KNOCK.
WHO'S THERE?
ALTHEA.
ALTHEA WHO?
ALTHEA LATER ALLIGATOR!

JOKE 95

KNOCK, KNOCK.
WHO'S THERE?
AMISH.
AMISH WHO?
SO THAT'S WHY
YOU SMELL LIKE FEET.

JOKE 96

KNOCK, KNOCK
WHO'S THERE?
LEON.
LEON WHO?
LEON ME WHEN YOU'RE
NOT STRONG!

JOKE 97

KNOCK, KNOCK.
WHO'S THERE?
WATSON
WATSON WHO?
WATSON THE MENU
FOR DINNER?

JOKE 98

KNOCK, KNOCK.
WHO'S THERE?
BRUCE.
BRUCE WHO?
BRUCE EASILY,
DON'T HIT ME!

JOKE 99

KNOCK, KNOCK.
WHO'S THERE?
URINE.
URINE WHO?
URINE TROUBLE
IF YOU DON'T LET ME INSIDE!

JOKE 100

KNOCK, KNOCK.
WHO'S THERE?
VIPER.
VIPER WHO?
VIPER NOSE,
IT'S RUNNING.

JOKE 101

KNOCK KNOCK.
WHO'S THERE?
ROACH.
ROACH WHO?
ROACH YOU A TEXT.
DID YOU GET IT?

JOKE 102

KNOCK, KNOCK!
WHO'S THERE?
BEEZER.
BEEZER WHO?
BEEZER GOOD
AT MAKING HONEY.

JOKE 103

KNOCK, KNOCK.
WHO'S THERE?
POLICE.
POLICE WHO?
POLICE OPEN THE DOOR,
I'M COLD OUT HERE!

JOKE 104

KNOCK, KNOCK.
WHO'S THERE?
NOISE.
NOISE WHO?
NOISE OF YOU
TO LET ME IN.

JOKE 105

KNOCK, KNOCK.
WHO'S THERE?
PECAN!
PECAN WHO?
PECAN SOMEBODY
YOUR OWN SIZE!

JOKE 106

KNOCK, KNOCK.
WHO'S THERE?
CHICK!
CHICK WHO?
CHICK THE STOVE,
I SMELL SOMETHING
BURNING!

JOKE 107

KNOCK, KNOCK.
WHO'S THERE?
JUSTIN.
JUSTIN WHO?
JUSTIN THE NEIGHBORHOOD
AND CAME TO SAY HELLO!

JOKE 108

KNOCK, KNOCK.
WHO'S THERE?
HO-HO.
HO-HO WHO?
YOUR SANTA IMPRESSION
COULD USE SOME WORK.

JOKE 109

KNOCK, KNOCK.
WHO'S THERE?
BACON.
BACON WHO?
BACON YOU
A BIRTHDAY CAKE.

JOKE 110

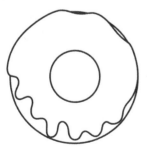

KNOCK, KNOCK.
WHO'S THERE?
DONUT.
DONUT WHO?
DONUT ASK ME
QUESTIONS LIKE THAT!

JOKE 111

KNOCK, KNOCK.
WHO'S THERE?
JESTER.
JESTER WHO?
JESTER SILLY KID!

JOKE 112

KNOCK, KNOCK.
WHO'S THERE?
YA
YA WHO?
I'M HAPPY
TO SEE YOU TOO!

JOKE 113

KNOCK, KNOCK.
WHO'S THERE?
VOODOO.
VOODOO WHO?
VOODOO YOU THINK YOU ARE,
ASKING ME SO MANY
QUESTIONS?

JOKE 114

KNOCK, KNOCK.
WHO'S THERE?
DIZZY.
DIZZY WHO?
DIZZY ME ROLLIN,
THEY HATIN'.

JOKE 115

KNOCK, KNOCK.
WHO'S THERE?
WATER?
WATER WHO?
WATER WAY TO ANSWER
THE DOOR!

JOKE 116

KNOCK, KNOCK.
WHO'S THERE?
DÉJA.
DÉJA WHO?
KNOCK KNOCK!

JOKE 117

KNOCK, KNOCK.
WHO'S THERE?
NEEDLE.
NEEDLE WHO?
NEEDLE LITTLE
HELP RIGHT NOW!

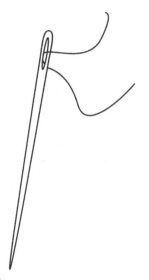

JOKE 118

KNOCK, KNOCK.
WHO'S THERE?
EARL.
EARL WHO?
EARL BE GLAD WHEN
YOU OPEN THE DOOR,
I'M COLD OUT HERE!

JOKE 119

KNOCK, KNOCK.
WHO'S THERE?
ALPACA.
ALPACA WHO?
ALPACA THE CAR,
YOU PACK THE SUITCASE.

JOKE 120

KNOCK, KNOCK
WHO'S THERE?
HIKE.
HIKE WHO?
I DIDN'T KNOW
YOU WERE A POETRY FAN!

JOKE 121

KNOCK, KNOCK.
WHO'S THERE?
ANITA
ANITA WHO?
ANITA BORROW A PEN.

JOKE 122

KNOCK, KNOCK.
WHO'S THERE?
PHONE.
PHONE WHO?
PHONELY I HAD A KEY
TO OPEN THE DOOR...

JOKE 123

KNOCK, KNOCK.
WHO'S THERE?
KEN.
KEN WHO?
KEN YOU COME
OUT TO PLAY?

JOKE 124

KNOCK, KNOCK!
WHO'S THERE?
SHAM.
SHAM WHO?
DID YOU JUST
CALL ME FAT?

KNOCK, KNOCK!
WHO'S THERE?
BERT.
BERT WHO?
BERT THE TOAST,
TRY AGAIN.

KNOCK, KNOCK.
WHO'S THERE?
CEREAL.
CEREAL WHO?
CEREAL PLEASURE
TO MEET YOU!

JOKE 127

KNOCK, KNOCK.
WHO'S THERE?
TENNIS.
TENNIS WHO?
TENNIS FIVE
PLUS FIVE!

JOKE 128

KNOCK, KNOCK!
WHO'S THERE?
HENRIETTA.
HENRIETTA WHO?
HENRIETTA SNAIL
THAT WAS IN HIS SALAD.

KNOCK, KNOCK.
WHO'S THERE?
CAESAR.
CAESAR WHO?
CAESAR QUICK,
SHE STOLE MY PURSE!

KNOCK, KNOCK.
WHO'S THERE?
HATCH.
HATCH WHO?
GOD BLESS YOU.

JOKE 131

KNOCK, KNOCK.
WHO'S THERE?
A LITTLE OLD LADY.
A LITTLE
OLD LADY WHO?
HEY, YOU CAN YODEL!

JOKE 132

KNOCK, KNOCK.
WHO'S THERE?
ZANY.
ZANY WHO?
ZANY BODY HOME?

JOKE 133

KNOCK, KNOCK.
WHO'S THERE?
KIWI.
KIWI WHO?
KIWI GO GET ICE CREAM?

JOKE 134

KNOCK, KNOCK.
WHO'S THERE?
ZOOM.
ZOOM WHO?
ZOOM DID YOU EXPECT!

JOKE 135

KNOCK, KNOCK.
WHO'S THERE?
ALMA.
ALMA WHO?
ALMA NOT GOING
TO TELL YOU.

JOKE 136

KNOCK, KNOCK.
WHO'S THERE?
PASSION.
PASSION WHO?
JUST PASSION BY
AND WANTED TO SAY HELLO!

JOKE 137

KNOCK, KNOCK.
WHO'S THERE?
HAMMOND.
HAMMOND WHO?
HAMMOND EGGS!

JOKE 138

KNOCK, KNOCK
WHO'S THERE?
A MAYAN.
A MAYAN WHO?
A MAYAN IN YOUR WAY?

JOKE 139

KNOCK, KNOCK
WHO'S THERE?
SAYS.
SAYS WHO?
SAYS ME, THAT'S WHO!

JOKE 140

KNOCK, KNOCK
WHO'S THERE?
IRAN.
IRAN WHO?
IRAN OVER TO TELL
YOU THIS JOKE!

JOKE 141

KNOCK, KNOCK.
WHO'S THERE?
SHERLOCK.
SHERLOCK WHO?
SHERLOCK YOUR
DOORS AT NIGHT.

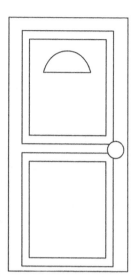

JOKE 142

KNOCK, KNOCK.
WHO'S THERE?
DOUBLE.
DOUBLE WHO?
W!

KNOCK, KNOCK
WHO'S THERE?
KENYA.
KENYA WHO?
KENYA FEEL THE LOVE
TONIGHT?

KNOCK, KNOCK.
WHO'S THERE?
OTTO.
OTTO WHO?
OTTO KNOW WHAT'S
TAKING YOU SO
LONG TO LET ME IN!

JOKE 145

KNOCK, KNOCK.
WHO'S THERE?
BROKEN PENCIL.
BROKEN PENCIL WHO?
FORGET IT, THERE'S
NO POINT!

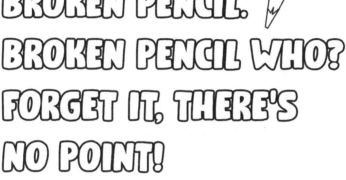

JOKE 146

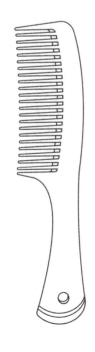

KNOCK, KNOCK.
WHO'S THERE?
COMB.
COMB WHO?
COMB ON DOWN
AND I'LL TELL YOU!

JOKE 147

KNOCK, KNOCK.
WHO'S THERE?
BOO.
BOO WHO?
AW, DON'T CRY!

JOKE 148

KNOCK, KNOCK.
WHO'S THERE?
TERESA.
TERESA WHO?
TERESA HAVE LEAVES!

JOKE 149

KNOCK, KNOCK.
WHO'S THERE?
FIGS.
FIGS WHO?
FIGS YOUR DOORBELL
AND I WON'T HAVE
TO KNOCK!

JOKE 150

KNOCK, KNOCK.
WHO'S THERE?
ICING.
ICING WHO?
ICING SO LOUD,
THE WHOLE NEIGHBORHOOD
CAN HEAR.

JOKE 151

KNOCK, KNOCK.
WHO'S THERE?
BARBARA.
BARBARA WHO?
BARBARA BLACK SHEEP,
HAVE YOU ANY WOOL...

JOKE 152

KNOCK, KNOCK.
WHO'S THERE?
BUDDHA.
BUDDHA WHO?
BUDDHA THIS SLICE
OF BREAD FOR ME!

JOKE 153

KNOCK, KNOCK.
WHO'S THERE?
WITCH
WITCH WHO?
WITCH ONE OF YOU
IS GOING TO WATCH
A MOVIE WITH ME?

JOKE 154

KNOCK, KNOCK.
WHO'S THERE?
HAL.
HAL WHO?
HAL WILL YOU KNOW
IF YOU DON'T
OPEN THE DOOR?

JOKE 155

KNOCK, KNOCK!
WHO'S THERE?
TARZAN.
TARZAN WHO?
TARZAN STRIPES FOREVER.

JOKE 156

KNOCK, KNOCK.
WHO'S THERE?
FLEA.
FLEA WHO?
FLEA BLIND MICE!

JOKE 157

KNOCK, KNOCK.
WHO'S THERE?
NANA.
NANA WHO?
NANA YOUR BUSINESS
WHO'S THERE.

JOKE 158

KNOCK, KNOCK.
WHO'S THERE?
BEETS!
BEETS WHO?
BEETS ME!

JOKE 159

KNOCK, KNOCK!
WHO'S THERE?
ADAIR.
ADAIR WHO?
ADAIR ONCE BUT
NOW I'M BALD.

JOKE 160

KNOCK, KNOCK
WHO'S THERE?
AMOS.
AMOS WHO?
A MOSQUITO!

JOKE 161

KNOCK, KNOCK
WHO'S THERE?
DISHES.
DISHES WHO?
DISHES THE FBI, OPEN UP!

JOKE 162

KNOCK, KNOCK.
WHO'S THERE?
KETCHUP.
KETCHUP WHO?
KETCHUP WITH ME
AND MAYBE I'LL TELL YOU!

JOKE 163

KNOCK, KNOCK.
WHO'S THERE?
RADIO.
RADIO WHO?
RADIO NOT, HERE I COME.

JOKE 164

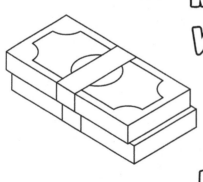

KNOCK, KNOCK
WHO'S THERE?
RAZOR.
RAZOR WHO?
RAZOR HANDS
AND SHOW ME THE MONEY!

JOKE 165

KNOCK, KNOCK.
WHO'S THERE?
GINO.
GINO WHO?
GINO ME OR NOT,
NOW OPEN THE DOOR!

JOKE 166

KNOCK, KNOCK.
WHO'S THERE?
MANGO!
MANGO WHO?
MAN-GO ANSWER
THE DOOR ALREADY!

JOKE 167

KNOCK, KNOCK!
WHO'S THERE?
BULLET.
BULLET WHO?
BULLET ALL THE HAY
AND NOW IT'S ALL GONE!

JOKE 168

KNOCK, KNOCK.
WHO'S THERE?
PEAS
PEAS WHO?
PEAS PASS THE GRAVY.

JOKE 169

KNOCK, KNOCK.
WHO'S THERE?
JOE.
JOE WHO?
JOE AWAY,
I'M NOT TALKING TO YOU.

JOKE 170

KNOCK, KNOCK.
WHO'S THERE?
LEASH.
LEASH WHO?
LEASH YOU COULD
DO IS LET ME IN!

JOKE 171

KNOCK, KNOCK.
WHO'S THERE?
BEEHIVE.
BEEHIVE WHO?
BEEHIVE YOURSELF
OR YOU WILL GET
INTO TROUBLE.

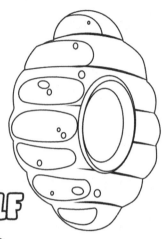

JOKE 172

KNOCK, KNOCK.
WHO'S THERE?
WIRE.
WIRE WHO?
WIRE YOU LOOKING
AT ME?

JOKE 173

KNOCK, KNOCK.
WHO'S THERE?
TURNIP.
TURNIP WHO?
TURNIP THE MUSIC,
IT'S TOO QUIET!

JOKE 174

KNOCK, KNOCK.
WHO'S THERE?
OAKHAM.
OAKHAM WHO?
OAKHAM ALL YE FAITHFUL,
JOYFUL AND TRIUMPHANT...

JOKE 175

KNOCK, KNOCK.
WHO'S THERE?
IVOR.
IVOR WHO?
IVOR YOU OPEN UP OR
I'LL CRAWL THROUGH
THE WINDOW.

JOKE 176

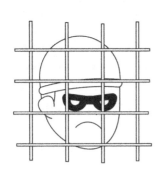

KNOCK, KNOCK.
WHO'S THERE?
KERMIT.
KERMIT WHO?
KERMIT A CRIME
AND YOU'LL GO TO JAIL!

JOKE 177

KNOCK, KNOCK.
WHO'S THERE?
LETTUCE.
LETTUCE WHO?
LETTUCE IN IT'S COLD
OUTSIDE!

JOKE 178

KNOCK, KNOCK.
WHO'S THERE?
BEN.
BEN WHO?
BEN STANDING HERE
FOR 10 MINUTES.
LET ME IN!

JOKE 179

KNOCK, KNOCK.
WHO'S THERE?
GORILLA.
GORILLA WHO?
GORILLA ME A HOTDOG.

JOKE 180

KNOCK, KNOCK.
WHO'S THERE?
ADORE.
ADORE WHO?
ADORE IS IN THE WAY.
OPEN UP!

JOKE 181

KNOCK, KNOCK.
WHO'S THERE?
GLADYS.
GLADYS WHO?
GLADYS THE WEEKEND,
NO SCHOOL!

JOKE 182

KNOCK, KNOCK.
WHO'S THERE?
OLIVE.
OLIVE WHO?
OLIVE YOU!

JOKE 183

KNOCK, KNOCK.
WHO'S THERE?
ISABEL.
ISABEL WHO?
ISABEL WORKING?
I HAD TO KNOCK.

JOKE 184

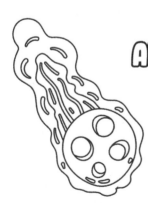

KNOCK, KNOCK.
WHO'S THERE?
ARMAGEDDON.
ARMAGEDDON WHO?
ARMAGEDDON
A LITTLE HUNGRY.
WANT TO MAKE
ME SOME FOOD?

JOKE 185

KNOCK, KNOCK!
WHO'S THERE?
NACHO.
NACHO WHO?
NACHO CHEESE!

JOKE 186

KNOCK, KNOCK.
WHO'S THERE?
KENT.
KENT WHO?
KENT YOU TELL WHO
I AM BY MY VOICE?

JOKE 187

KNOCK, KNOCK
WHO'S THERE?
SWEDEN.
SWEDEN WHO?
SWEDEN SOUR CHICKEN!

JOKE 188

KNOCK, KNOCK.
WHO'S THERE?
ALEC.
ALEC WHO?
ALECTRICITY. BUZZ!

JOKE 189

KNOCK, KNOCK!
WHO'S THERE?
AARDVARK.
AARDVARK WHO?
AARDVARK A HUNDRED
MILES TO SEE YOU!

JOKE 190

KNOCK, KNOCK.
WHO'S THERE?
YUGO.
YUGO WHO?
YUGO FIRST AND
I'LL FOLLOW.

JOKE 191

KNOCK, KNOCK.
WHO'S THERE?
MIKEY
MIKEY WHO?
MIKEY ISN'T WORKING,
CAN YOU LET ME IN?

JOKE 192

KNOCK, KNOCK!
WHO'S THERE?
BISON.
BISON WHO?
BISON POPCORN
FOR THE MOVIE!

JOKE 193

KNOCK, KNOCK.
WHO'S THERE?
SNOW.
SNOW WHO?
SNOW USE.
I LOST MY KEYS.

JOKE 194

KNOCK, KNOCK!
WHO'S THERE?
CHER.
CHER WHO?
CHER-LOCK HOLMES.

JOKE 195

KNOCK, KNOCK!
WHO'S THERE?
BENJAMIN.
BENJAMIN WHO?
BENJAMIN
TO THE MUSIC.

JOKE 196

KNOCK, KNOCK.
WHO'S THERE?
IVA.
IVA WHO?
I'VE A SORE HAND
FROM KNOCKING
FOR SO LONG!

JOKE 197

KNOCK, KNOCK!
WHO'S THERE?
FREEZE.
FREEZE WHO?
FREEZE A JOLLY
GOOD FELLOW!

JOKE 198

KNOCK, KNOCK.
WHO'S THERE?
AMY.
AMY WHO?
AMY FRAID I'VE
FORGOTTEN!

JOKE 199

KNOCK, KNOCK.
WHO'S THERE?
THEODORE!
THEODORE WHO?
THEODORE WAS LOCKED,
SO I KNOCKED.

JOKE 200

KNOCK, KNOCK.
WHO'S THERE?
MUSTACHE.
MUSTACHE WHO?
I MUSTACHE YOU A QUESTION,
BUT I'LL SHAVE
IT FOR ANOTHER TIME.

JOKE 201

KNOCK, KNOCK!
WHO'S THERE?
KANGA.
KANGA WHO?
NO, KANGAROO!

JOKE 202

KNOCK, KNOCK.
WHO'S THERE?
PUDDING.
PUDDING WHO?
PUDDING ON SHOES
BEFORE SOCKS IS A BAD IDEA!

JOKE 203

KNOCK, KNOCK.
WHO'S THERE?
ICE CREAM.
ICE CREAM WHO?
ICE CREAM IF WE DON'T
GET ICE CREAM!

JOKE 204

KNOCK, KNOCK.
WHO'S THERE?
GRUB.
GRUB WHO?
GRUB MY HAND
AND LET'S GO!

JOKE 205

KNOCK, KNOCK.
WHO'S THERE?
YUKON.
YUKON WHO?
YUKON SAY
THAT AGAIN!

JOKE 206

KNOCK, KNOCK.
WHO'S THERE?
I EAT MOP.
I EAT MOP WHO?
GROSS!

JOKE 207

KNOCK, KNOCK.
WHO'S THERE?
TWO KNEE.
TWO KNEE WHO?
TWO-KNEE FISH!

JOKE 208

KNOCK, KNOCK.
WHO'S THERE?
BEEF.
BEEF WHO?
BEFORE I COME IN,
WHAT SNACKS
DO YOU HAVE?

JOKE 209

KNOCK, KNOCK.
WHO'S THERE?
DORIS.
DORIS WHO?
DORIS LOCKED.
LET ME IN, PLEASE!

JOKE 210

KNOCK, KNOCK!
WHO'S THERE?
AMMONIA.
AMMONIA WHO?
AMMONIA LITTLE KID!

JOKE 211

KNOCK, KNOCK.
WHO'S THERE?
PASTA.
PASTA WHO?
PASTA BUTTER, PLEASE!

JOKE 212

KNOCK, KNOCK.
WHO'S THERE?
HOWARD.
HOWARD WHO?
HOWARD I KNOW?

JOKE 213

KNOCK, KNOCK.
WHO'S THERE?
LEE.
LEE WHO?
LEE ME ALONE!

JOKE 214

KNOCK, KNOCK.
WHO'S THERE?
WHO.
WHO WHO?
IS THERE AN OWL
IN HERE?

JOKE 215

KNOCK, KNOCK.
WHO'S THERE?
STOPWATCH
STOPWATCH WHO?
STOPWATCH YOU'RE DOING
AND DO THE BOOGIE!

JOKE 216

KNOCK, KNOCK!
WHO'S THERE?
FALAFEL.
FALAFEL WHO?
FALAFEL MY BIKE AND
SCRAPED MY LEG.

JOKE 217

KNOCK, KNOCK.
WHO'S THERE?
HEAVEN.
HEAVEN WHO?
HEAVEN SEEN YOU
IN AGES!

JOKE 218

KNOCK, KNOCK!
WHO'S THERE?
SUSAN.
SUSAN WHO?
SUSAN SOCKS
GO ON YOUR FEET.

JOKE 219

KNOCK, KNOCK.
WHO'S THERE?
RAY.
RAY WHO?
RAY-MEMBER ME?!

JOKE 220

KNOCK, KNOCK.
WHO'S THERE?
OZZIE.
OZZIE WHO?
OZZIE YOU LATER!